A Stroll for the Soul

A Book of Jewish Poems

ISBN: 9798526900256

For the courage it takes to keep the conversation going.

Special thanks to:

My dear parents

Zvi Fermaglich

Alexandra Chechik

Meirav Horak

Batsheva Lasky

Dear Reader,

I want to thank you for meeting me here. Whether you're new to the world of poetry or familiar, whether you're observant or not quite there, I made sure to include everyone. When conceiving the idea to write a poetry book about Jewish life, I knew I wasn't the first. Mountains of work are produced daily by myriads of talents, echoing King Solomon's wisdom, there is nothing new beneath the sun. Yet the commentary on the words in Genesis (18:27) "ואנכי עפר ואפר" - I am but dust and ashes, never fails to motivate my spirit because "בשבילי נברא העולם" - the world was created for me. Somehow there is always room for one more: song, painting, movement, soul to be set on fire. Nowadays there's an extraordinary desire for deeper thought and authentic talk. This is precisely what I've tried to tap into and accomplish, why every detail and decision was embedded with purpose. The book is divided into five sections corresponding to the חמישה חומשי תורה (Five Books of Moses) and is an acronym for *chaim*, meaning "life". The letters represent different aspects of Judaism to express its great nuance, nevertheless only once all of these parts are brought together can we truly be living. Consider this your soul's companion for when you need to laugh or cry or connect. I hope you find this book both enlightening and entertaining. I hope you discover questions and start conversations in pursuit of a more personal, meaningful Judaism. What I hope most is that you choose life and never fear the things you don't understand or don't feel. Trust the process and let the rest be.

Sincerely, Efrat

Dear Reader,

You are holding a delightful book of poems. The poems speak to an impressively wide spectrum of Jews and delves deeply into the religious and spiritual experiences of being a connected Jew. The stories will make you think, smile, wonder, feel sad, and appreciate the poignancy of the beautiful moments depicted. I particularly enjoyed how Efrat unabashedly celebrates naivete and joy, while also giving space to acknowledge the things she struggles with through her contemplations. This collection is nuanced, youthful, and generously descriptive. I hope that it will invite for you a new perspective. Reading these poems and depicting them reminded me of so many beautiful aspects of Judaism that I often take for granted. Efrat sees living a Jewish life as a constant gift and for her viewpoint, I am grateful.

With Love, Rebecca

Contents

Character~~~~~~~~~~~~~1

Holiness~~~~~~~~~~~~~~~~~29

Affection~~~~~~~~~~~~~~~~~~~~~57

Injury~~~~~~~~~~~~~~~~~~~~~~~~~~83

Mind~~~~~~~~~~~~~~~~~~~~~~~~~~~~~~~111

Section I

Character

From its inception, Jewish culture has been a multifaceted and resilient force. Although its details have changed over the millennia, its faithful interaction with us has not. It has formed the complex and familiar character we have come to proudly recognize wherever we go. In this section, you will uncover layers and links that make our bond strong. You will see that the Jewish personality is not a "one size fits all". It is tailored to the individual as one grows while meshing miraculously well with the whole, fashioning a people unlike any other.

Today

Today is the day
for you to choose
not to dwell among the 1%
of neutrality, negativity
you may consume and
be consumed by.
Now is the time
for you to decide
to live with the 99%
of goodness, G-dliness
you may breathe in and
have breathed into you
upon walking this way.

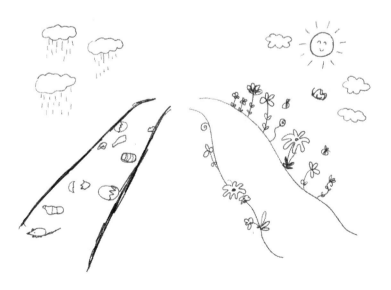

Responsibilities

We have two hands for a reason
while one does the dirty work
the other does the cleaning

-kol yisrael areivim zeh l'zeh

The WhatsApp Chat

Depending on the day, my *tefillah* statuses sway:

1. Sent, not delivered

    ~ angels off duty, probably having a holiday

2. Delivered, not read

    ~ I could wait knowing it reached the front gate

3. Read, not replied

    ~ I'm getting somewhere at least, right?

4. Read and replied

    ~ BEST.DAY.EVER

5. Neither sent nor delivered

    ~ hardest day ever

5

Carbs & Protein

The secret to Jewish success?
The challah and the hummus.
The kugel and the cholent.

The most righteous of pairs.

-hatzlacha u'bracha

The Best Friend

You spend quality time by the Kugels for shabbos,
party with the Latkes for eight nights of chanukah.
Soon duty calls you to anoint the Kings of Israel
and later to aid the *Kohen Gadol* in his *avodah*.

You're soaked into the fabric of every function,
a real champion at Jewish geography and history.
The friend who knows our secrets' secrets & is there
through all the thick schnitzel and the thin ones too.

-oil

The Great Debate

The caffeine in a morning cup charging till sundown.
The kick in a modest step teaching of *chutzpah*.
The spice in a dish setting warm mouths ablaze.

You button press every space, letter, word and punctuation
because you know we never settle for the black and white.
We love grays, we create shades of them any chance there is,
splatter them across the canvas of Jewish life and call it truth,
a masterpiece, a miracle if we ever agree on what we later see.

-Machloket L'Shem Shamayim

Are You?

The one word operating as a noun, adjective, verb, and escape key all to avoid answering the awkward "*shomer*" question honestly. Four letters charming its way into spaces that forget to make room for its many defining faces.

Shabbos Walks

At midnight I often crave
for a spiritual tidal wave
to blanket, soften my soul's edge
take me on a walk to remember
with Hashem & renew our pledge

-hitbodedut

Only Simchas!

Ten vendors
Nine bridesmaids
Eight arches
Seven *brachot*
Six hours
Five shots
Four dances
Three courses
Two witnesses
One happy couple

-Jewish weddings

11

Sweet Tooth

doughy cheeks
noodle *payis*
vanilla smiles
buttery voices
creamy ponytails
sprinkled eyes
crunchy *yarmulkes*
juicy freckles
bite-sized

-borough park *kinderlach*

Her Majesty

The wrinkles give grace
white strands grant wisdom
accent upon her lips like lace
the Queen of a mighty kingdom

She may not look like it all day
when cooped up at home alone
but She has stories to convey
from her time on the throne

-Savta

13

L'Chaim

The drink of life is
sipping
spilling
slipping
and still
standing up
to raise a cup

A Volleyball Game

Warning:
it will hit you in the face at first
you may hesitate to hit back
but once you learn the rules
of the volleys and the spikes
just keep the ball in the air
and make sure to have fun!

(observing is a blast too)

-Jewish/Israeli bargaining

Shoko B'Sakit

A dream whipped up in the milky way
sent down to earth in a baggie
making an unparalleled universe
portable
and Monday mornings
manageable

The Gap Year

An American wand in an Israeli bottle
blowing bubbles of *achdus*
main ingredient: *chavayot*

-yeshiva/seminary

17

Jewish Grammar

A guide for when to apply rules:
Comma – trying to catch up to the rabbi's pace, accompanying hand motions, and shiur you just walked into late
Period – stopping yourself mid-snooze, or mid-daydream, from drifting off in order to focus on the speaker at the podium
Exclamation Point – finding the rabbi's *chidush* profoundly life-changing, making you rush to jot it down in its entirety
Question Mark – a corny joke not fitting well within the context, or the rabbi innocently going off on a tangent
Dash – paying super close attention now as the rabbi answers a challenging question made by a *charif* kid
Quotation Marks – pretending to repeat the rabbi's idea verbatim after someone asks you for it, though you spaced out in that moment
Capitalization – needing the confidence to make a remark, you sit up straight, raise your hand and hope it comes out right when called
Apostrophe – feeling the lesson connect on a personal level, proving Hashem never forgot about you and is constantly reaching out
Parentheses – the rabbi adding a controversial twist or comical side comment, said loudly yet softly so few could hear
Semi-Colon – the shiur is over but there's one person who must always have a question while winding down, and it starts all over again,.!?--"J')(;

The Babysitter

Babysitting is the *derech* of every:
12-year-old to cash in on late wedding nights
13-year-old to cash in on evening college classes
14-year-old to cash in on romantic date nights
15-year-old to cash in on morning errands
16-year-old to cash in on business trips
17-year-old to cash in on holiday programs
18-year-old to cash in on anything & everything

It is the sitter who gives society a smooth run,
a fast sprint down any chosen *derech*.
V'*zakeini l'gadel* babysitter *u'vnei* babysitter –
and may we be blessed to know their *erech*!

Unpopular Opinion

I truly savor my matzah bits
for it has the crunch of a cracker
the print of a cheetah
and the taste of a timeless
Jewish experience

The Dilemma

Cream cheese or chocolate spread?
       tuna or jam?
Peanut butter or some plain butter?

-matzah sandwich

Desserts Galore!

Friday, as the clock gallops toward midnight, the candy land of your wildest imagination rides through. It tugs at your fingertips and table tops. A ceremony unfolds crowning you the Candy Queen or King. A royal treatment escorts you until the brim of tomorrow's dusk. I only pray shame doesn't coup the cravings. 'Tis a sweet reign shaking off the shackles of guilt, redeeming those sweat-filled six days. You see, it is only befitting to overthrow the celery and surrender to the calorie.

-oneg shabbat

Shabbos Naps

In a galaxy far away
where worries go
to drift and dream,
where solutions awaken
put stresses to slumber,
where a surface reality
submits to a deep serenity,
that is where G-d's satellite and mine meet.

The Grocery List

If acquiring *middot* could be done with a trip to the grocery store, we'd check out as tzaddikim.

You first walk in to see *anavah* by the bread, because the success of your kitchen starts with an inner humility.
Continuing to the dairy aisle, a fine, "fat-free" cheesecake waits for *zerizut* to kick in but is snatched by another right before the taking. Miraculously, with some serious *ratzon*, you find a quiet one in the back wrapped in cool air.
Then the sweets angelically call your name with *ahavah*. How can you not reciprocate? It's love at first sight and bite.
Simcha - you spot it with the biggest smile in the fruits and veggies section since you couldn't be more pleased to shed those post-*chagim* pounds.
Your dear friend *reut* swiftly enters the scene as you pass the aisle of miscellaneous Judaica, offering only the best manufactured chachkas around. Although you threw away an apartment full of them last Pesach, you promise it'll be different this time.
Now *yirah* sets in as you tiptoe past the frozen hierarchy of ice creams and quick dinners.
Finally, *temidiyut* tests your limits at the cashier with candy bars and gums winking at your wallet. But you brush them off without a sweat and call it a day – a great grocery done day.
It's a happy *shalom* until your next visit to the store – tomorrow!

B'tzelem Elokim

You were crafted carefully
made perfectly imperfect
so you best
style that stitch
model that mark
flaunt that flaw

you are forever in vogue

-From the Chief Designer's Desk

25

The Three *Avot*

You got a brain at the top
a heart in the middle
and feet at the bottom.

A hand for stop
some fingers that fiddle
all set now, go out and get em'.

-kiruv

Airbnb

Who needs an Airbnb when you've got
Jewish brothers and sisters
gift-wrapped around the globe?

The *Shylah*

Early morning or late night
when found wrong or right
this is what we commonly do.
It's the tradition of every Jew
guiding us to an eternal truth,
practicing through early youth.
Questions upon questions are what we ask,
it is deeply ingrained, a second-nature task.
No matter how small, odd, or complex,
book & brain muscles we surely do flex.
There is a set time to learn, grow, and inspire,
but when hitting bumps on the page – inquire.
A cycle that keeps on going,
a *neshama* brightly glowing.
A question placed in the palm as playdough, pull & twist in a
desired direction.
Asking even one out of the millions steers you closer to the
ultimate Perfection.
I mean – haven't you ever heard that a Jew answers a question
with a question?

Section II

Holiness

Esoteric and intimidating is what it sometimes feels like, but a holy mindset does not discriminate between hosts. It embraces all lives, enriches them in ways beyond our comprehension. Though the Torah's commandments can be challenging, their purpose is not to deny nor detach us from reality. They're meant to reveal and develop our inner divinity to better society. In this section, you will experience a more elevated and reflective Judaism. It may even inspire the holy spark within to make its debut. Your Yiddishkeit just wants to meet where you are and hopes you'll want to do the same.

Thank You

Modeh ani
i thank Thee:

upon waking
and
seeing
and
sitting
and
speaking
and
standing
and
stretching
and
walking
and
washing
and
dressing
and
thinking
and
praying
and
eating
and
blessing
and
living
soulfully

-counting my blessings

The Vision Test

Picture him wearing a black hat & conquering the basketball court.
Picture her wearing a tee and shorts & leading the shabbat *zmirot*.
Picture him wearing faded, ripped jeans & being the first at *neitz*.
Picture her wearing a pleated maxi skirt & passionately reciting rap.
Picture him wearing a *shtreimel* & writing, directing Hollywood films.
Picture her wearing body piercings & strictly following *Rabbeinu Tam*.
Picture him wearing a man bun & hosting large, Glatt kosher meals.
Picture her wearing neutral tones & making statements with each step.
Picture him wearing sleek *peot* with *tzitzit* out & serving in the IDF.
Picture her wearing gossip & giving loads to charity anonymously.
Picture him wearing animal tattoos & committing to Friday mikvahs.
Picture her wearing a *mitpachat*, siddur in hand, & running for office.

They're not your picture-perfect Jew, but is anyone? We are uniquely colored gemstones set within the mosaic of our nationhood, made more stunning when brought together in unity. While it can communicate, what we wear is not who we are. Our actions speak louder than our words and wardrobes.

-havay dan et kol adam l'kaf z'chut

Listen Closely

your mute is the loudest riot
begging to be heard by the masses
revolutionizing what it means to speak
not through the canals of *lashon hara*
but through the echoes of its silence

Jewish History

The spanning of generations
spun by the divine spindle
drawn by a thread of faith
weaving together *neshamot*
making a national *ketonet*
kaleidoscopic
owned not by any history.

A voice from the past is raised
heard louder with each telling
over of chapters on the family
written in warm blood, heart
that keeps beating on every time
the page is turned and read aloud.

Jerusalem

A city covered in golden freckles
with eyes warm as mother's
and arms wide as father's
welcoming me home once again
to the kingdom of my soul
with lions lined up ready
to roar upon my arrival

Holiday Season

As my rabbi in seminary used to say,
chagim are the gas stations along the way
a holiday special, spiritual protein whey
filling up our tanks with renewed energy
from our lavish meals to our holy liturgy
adding spice to the temperate, ordinary.

A Blissful Night

Walking beside trees harmonized by summer,
looping right around a spacious crisp corner.
Chiseling silver stars upon a sapphire backdrop
pinned high, a wrinkle-free sky stretched on top.
Making stiff necks turn, matte eyes twinkle
as stardust graciously goes on to sprinkle.

Beauty sweeps, twines in tender air
introducing hearts to a path so rare.
The breeze humbles in tone, curves smoothly on cheeks
a leaf blows by, softly parachutes down from trees' peaks.

Though quiet, there are greetings between street signs
applauding the moment for how it perfectly fits & aligns.
At this hour the city lights calmly dim, night takes the win
for faithfulness
filtering in bliss out of a day's blister, swapping sun for moon
with no bitterness.

-shavuot night

The Sea of Halacha

It's not a competition to come up with the most complex.
It's seeking all that is hidden
waiting to be held in the minds and hands of those
willing to smash the glass doors and ceilings
witness their crystals free falling into the streams of time
calling on shallow banks to rise, shadowed facets to shine,
and to illuminate a more accurate reality
reflecting back and connecting forward

-chidush

People of the Book

They call us the people of the book but:
if they look close, they'll find texts stretching and sprinting freely
if they look closer, they'll discover faith speaking its mind frankly
if they look closest, they'll see a furrowed brow moving fearlessly
working to assemble the puzzle with other master players
spanning centuries.

They partake in the search for the right pieces and celebrate in
their union. Once a section is complete, its animation becomes
more visible & magical. Maybe we are the people of the book but,
we're also the people of the most clever & creative treasure hunt
ever mapped out.

Let it Pour

Mitzvot are like tiny raindrops rushing down to bathe earth's cradle, to soften the concrete in man. It's the water observed by Rabbi Akiva, dripping on to the rock in our everyday lives. As if pieces of *shamayim* come packaged in droplets, subtle yet impactful. They're not easy to grasp and at times leave us in an awkward spot, that one between the rain and shine where all we feel is damp. Though if this is the weather forecast for redemption, let the rain come pouring down.

Let them drown out the naysayers and evildoers. Let them create ripples in puddles and puddles in ripples, inspiring leaps of faith in their neighboring pools. Let these drops huddle us closer under one umbrella. Let them teach us how to sing and skip in the rain. Let them soak us in forgiveness and shower us with blessings. Let these raindrops tap-dance on the windows of the sleepy. Let those splashes be bits of light crashing into streets, sparking hope everywhere. Let these drops wash away our coffee-stained structures and make us bows to its rain; for *mitzvot* with rainbow residue will only wax, not wane.

Jewish Sounds

That mighty *shofar* blow on Rosh Hashana
That coin drop to the bottom of the *pushka*
That beautifully moving *Hatikvah* melody
That soft and pure, pre-school *modeh ani*
That musically in sync, inspiring *havdalah*
That awesome and roaring "*shanah habah*"

That *bracha* said aloud and a crowd-filled "amen"
That familiar tapping of *Saba*'s old and wise cane
That crinkling foil covering all shabbat food
That soft *tefillah* murmur, molding a *Kotel* mood
That modest voice, a bar-mitzvah boy's first *layn*
That rowdy *chavrusa* working the other's brain

That rustling shake of *arba'at haminim*
That intense unity, cheerful Adar theme
That sweet bedtime "*hamalach hagoel*"
That hyped voice in the *shuk* trying to sell
That Israeli taxi talk, just blowing off steam
That Breslov truck, music shaking every beam

Jewish Sights

That stroll of young & old along Ben Yehuda
That long bakery line for shabbos challah
That simchat hatorah throwing of candy
That JFK parting for yeshiva or seminary
That unique painting sparked by kabbalah
That lengthy yet always meaningful *chuppah*

That *kiddush levana* outdoor gathering
That talmid *chaping*, mishnah mastering
That couple & carriage on a shabbos walk
That *morah* giving the class a *mussar* talk
That sukkah construction and hammering
That salon full for pre-shabbos pampering

That minyan at theme parks, *chol hamoed* trips
That family at a restaurant leaving nice tips
That *bubby* smothering, spoiling their grandkid
That *zaidy* at shul raising each congregant's bid
That quiet shuckle in shul, movement of lips
That one running to help when a person slips

Jewish Smells

That Lag Ba'Omer, smokey laundry load
That vital Yom Kippur *besamim* borrowed
That perfumed air, entering an Israeli mall
That Purim table with much spilled alcohol
That matzah ball soup, senses overload
That tuna sandwich when on the road

That spring bloom in Israel, a beautiful cliche
That Turkish coffee brewed fresh for the day
That wrinkled *siddur*, pages with a distinct note
That burning of *chametz* filling your throat
That Friday kitchen, making meals gourmet
That Israeli fabric softener, heaven in a spray

That rich cholent on shabbat, leaving a trace
That fallen sukkot rain, earth's pure embrace
That wax dripping from the chanukah menorah
That visit to the elderly, a warm and wise aura
That showering & ironing, another pre-*chag* race
That BBQ for *Yom Ha'atzmaut*, celebratory space

Jewish Tastes

That crunchy, unleavened Pesach bread
That bagel at a *bris* with a dairy spread
That falafel, chips & salad in a pita combo
That *heimish* spinoff of the classic Oreo
That bitter sweat of all those who have fled
That dry and stale mouth, Tisha B'Av dread

That tea steaming early shabbat morning
That burned challah corner worth munching
That seder with viscous *charoset*, homemade
That gefilte with carrots and horseradish laid
That crisp apple with honey on its side gliding
That kosher airplane food, tastes coinciding

That fried schnitzel, oil bursting through each pore
That Mizrahi dish made with colorful spices galore
That Bissli residue left on fingertips, you lick clean
That dead sea salt on the tongue, a sting so mean
That desert dust hiking Masada, settling in your core
That cheesecake with caramel, just one piece more

Jewish Feels

That silky landing, touching Israel's ground
That soulful vibe in Tzfat flowing around
That *hagbah* moment in shul infusing pride
That childhood friend, now soon-to-be bride
That special *pasuk* for a lost item, said & found
That hopeful belief shabbos cancels the pound

That interior designer debut for sukkah decorating
That long Yom Kippur *amidah*, feet muscles aching
That kneading and folding of *hamentaschen* dough
That IDF pride, protecting a place for us to always go
That *Yom Yerushalayim* smush of people parading
That late-night babysitting gig, a test run in parenting

That tight hug from clothes, a shabbat meal so vast
That *hashgacha pratit* story, faith made steadfast
That *birkat kohanim* at the *Kotel*, as one body we pray
That *gematria* blowing your mind dimensions away
That bat-mitzvah energy, dancing to beats that blast
That 2,000-year-old realized dream – at last!

Yom Ha'atzmaut

A land drizzled in milk and honey, a bitter yet blissful flowing of fate.
A song ringing around her people, adorned in reasons that celebrate.
A country drenched in politics and the pursuit of a destined soulmate.
A sighting of life among rubble, where millions of docked dreams await.
A state rising to the occasion & story those indigenous resume to narrate.

-1948

Good vs. Great

Anyone can actualize their greatness.
The challenge is finding those who can realize their goodness.

-nekuda tova

The Giver

As your life force gives, the richer your fuel gets & thicker greatness drips.
Capable of powering to the sun & moon a fleet of NASA spaceships.
That act of stripping from your nucleus always boomerangs back.
Trust that kindness will catch up to you & overflow parts that lack.

Before humanity knew how to host a self of another stripe, it ran
undomesticated.
Since then we've learned to hand and have, become one being -
consummated.
To give is to trace those divine specks trailing behind the Giver of
everything.
It's to collect the crumbs of every day until they become a plate worth
offering.

A universe bursting into colorful works of light, expanding the
brilliance of all
each time you water and shine another, making the galaxy grow
a little more tall.

-*chesed*

48

The Stroll

Flashes of wonder
streak through as it wanders,
the stroll my soul takes
is one that must deeply ponder,
am I connected to some greater thing
or will it end without the credits rolling?
On days filled with more sunsets than possible,
is there a hush sunrise reaching for the horizon
waiting to saturate my core, help answer
what do I live for?
My soul so badly wants to braid into all
that is breathing and have oneness tie,
marry the moment and open up to the sky.
The hands of time may run off without notice
but these fierce fingers will pick up in resilience
to prove the miracle of me and You
to reveal what *is* that must be true.

Let There Be Light

Be that firefly lighting up
someone's pitch black
backyard at 2 a.m.
"Vayehi or" was spoken
in coded language
with layered meanings.
Be the one who finds them in action
and never loses them in translation.

A Paradox

The *mechitzah:*

separates physically
connects spiritually

causes confusion
solves issues

feels intolerant
fosters freedom

breaks barriers
by building one

only by being apart
can we truly be together

R-E-S-P-E-C-T

Times are tough these days
for a lifelong debt accumulates
adding up on our statement
no matter how much is repaid.
The balance is way out of balance
consumerism has eaten us alive
we've lost touch with our makers.

Their wisdom has been diluted by the passing price tags.
The only solution is to walk in their footsteps, even if not
perfectly.
It will make room for reflection, and for respect most
importantly.

-Kibud Av V'Em

Moderation

Stuff is the enemy of the soul.
Too much of it makes you weary.
Too little of it makes you wonder.
Yet the little much of it makes you grateful.

-gashmiyut

Shabbos Vibes

Throats gulping down the thought of food right before the serving.
Eyes glowing, fully charged for the scene about to batter up and hit.
Kiddush perfectly pitched that chandeliers blush, glow brighter.
Homemade challah then cut and passed around with a posed civility.
It's the shabbos meal dominating your essence, smearing senses
as the dips on challah always do, a Picasso dream coming true.

-TGIF

Coming

we are in a constant state of becoming
and overcoming
though only when embracing a pause
choosing a rock to rest on
can we feel the rumble
of an inner homecoming

-teshuva

The Royal Family

Members serving His Majesty
Members courting infinity
Members recording history
Members crowning spirituality
Members honoring comradery
Members glorifying morality
Members dignifying physicality
Members escorting Jewry
Members declaring liberty
Members treasuring the holy
There are 613 members in the royal family

Section III

Affection

Growing up we're taught three main, defining traits of the Jewish people are: *rachmanim* – merciful, *bayshanim* – shy/modest, and *gomlei chasadim* – performing acts of kindness. The common thread tells of a Jew's mission, which is to share their natural compassion and emotional intelligence with the world. In this section, you might find yourself extra sentimental. As Jews, we don't shy away from our feelings. We're one, big family with enough love and drama to pass down for generations. It is this warmth that has gotten us through the coldest days of exile and what will, G-d willing, usher in the Mashiach.

The Chosen Conversation

G-d chose us
we chose Him back
it's a mutual relationship

G-d super swiped us
we swiped right in return
it's a match made in heaven

G-d hugged us
we hugged back
it's a love gifted on the *har*

G-d called us
we answered *"na'aseh v'nishma"*
it's a covenant alongside a conversation

You and G-d have matched!

Yin Yang

information in our heads
interlocking hands with
emotion in our hearts

-Torah *Sh'Beal Peh U'Bichtav*

Eye Contact

A tendency we can fail at often.
The world would be a different place
if we knew how to look at our prayers
in the eyes
of our *mitzvot*
in the eyes
of our *chavrusa, talmid, rebbe*
in the eyes
of our mothers, fathers, siblings
in the eyes
of Hashem.

It's not isolating eye contact
but securing soul contact.

Mashiach

deep in the cracks of the *nefesh* there simmers
a recipe for the deadliest poison, worst madness
to become a medicine stirring within its crevices
so the inner mashiach can ignite its own genesis

-salvation lives in you

Soul Sisters

Fonts, always enhancing a word's look
never fighting over who wore it best
or who made the most decorated book.
They unite lines & curves from east to west,
rejoice on the page as they break through margins,
give volume to a quiet language not foreign to
the heart's cocoon, & with every sentence it thins
showing the butterfly another way through.
With arms spread like wings, the fonts fly off papers
dissolve accents & spaces between to find soul sisters.

-International Jewish Women

Silver vs. Gold

silver and gold
bronze and brass
melded from them
the shield we wield
before countless histories
that saw past every contrast
aimed at the strong and the sore
showing us it's not a battle or enemy
but the army we fight with and for

-various *eidot*

Elעל Al אל Flights

The greatest love-hate relationship
that reels in refugees
and rolls out relatives

הכי בבית בעולם-

Post-Israel Trip

Too many times I do this
on my flight returning
sculpted through 6,000 clouds.
Just when I get over the jet lag
my clever soul comes up with
something to step in its place.
Like one sneeze after the other
when starting, there's no stopping:

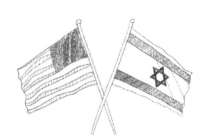

1.   Ordering Starbucks
confidently as an Aroma
"café kar"
2.   Swiping my Rav Kav at MTA subway stations
and on buses
3.   Seeing a Zoya sign instead of Zara boldly
hanging
4.   Saying *"slicha"* when passing people on narrow
sidewalks
5.   Spitting Hebrew slang with Anglo friends
having no clue
6.   Switching my phone's keyboard, on constant bi-
lingual mode
7.   Opening Moovit for a route I've done two
million times

With it all I recognize how lucky I am
to be
learning the 1776 history
and
living the 1948 reality

-*hakarat hatov* for the American-Israeli alliance

Shh

The most powerful moments pulsate when souls are still
praying between thunder or listening to another
remembering the survivors or hugging a brother
memorializing IDF soldiers or consoling a sister
a transformation occurs – once remote, now together

A Grateful Villanelle

There's nothing like the home I once knew
a child rolling in sugar and sunshine
swinging back and forth through air so sweet

Waking to sing with morning birds, each day anew
to loud growth and silent beauty, pure and fine
there's nothing like the home I once knew

Long, luscious pony tails and pony dolls too
playing, brushing each strand of theirs and mine
combing back and forth through locks so sweet

Fun fashion choices follow me through
late wedding nights, poufy dresses A-line
there's no place like the home I once knew

Daddy picking me up under a dome of blue
Mommy hugging me down in bed, each night at nine
swinging back and forth through days so sweet

Looking to my sister with eyes open and true
flashbacks wait for a greeting, patiently in line
there's nothing like the home I once knew
swinging back and forth, through life so sweet

-Hodu L'Hashem Ki Tov

Weak vs. Real

giving into feelings
is not weakness
you are in essence realness
you are what is called *emes*

Love

The only prescription you need, guaranteed.

-v'ahavta l'rayacha kamocha

Spiritual Recovery

i just want to hop into a hot air balloon and fly high away
spray paint the night sky with praises, filling each particle
unshadow demons from darkness and let my *zmirot* slay
slice through the ugly and replace it with Hashem's surgical
Hand patching scars, sewing me anew in His holiness, likeness

Mishpacha

Close your eyes and imagine:

- ~ wherever you go, you'll have a place to stay
- ~ whatever you do, you'll be loved and looked after
- ~ whenever you fall, you'll be caught and comforted
- ~ whether you leave or return, you'll always be welcomed

This is what it means to be a family, what it means to look at another Jew and feel that you've come home.

*especially when in the middle of nowhere

We're All in This Together

They are the soft and rugged palms
teaching what it takes to build
and be whole from the ground up.
They are the skyscraping souls
mesmerizing clouds and steadying soil
since they know when to level and lift the other.

-kehila

The Healthcare System

You are the healthcare providers, first responders, and
miracle workers for the Jewish mind, heart, and soul.
You are
the funds
the charities
the platforms
the federations
the institutions
the movements
the organizations
the collective individuals
You are, therefore, we are

-thank you

Superheroes

A hero
a man-made marvel rooted in the daily grinds,
hand-makes greatness with what's given,
and champions humanity by taking responsibility
to be super and help others be so too.
A hero sees beyond its own clothed back
to rescue the world from its nakedness,
tells it to suit up with capes made of capabilities,
so universal flight can have greater possibilities.

-light unto the nations

Olive Green

A color brewing home-made pride
thawing the great icebergs inside

צה"ל - uniform

I Got the Chills

I radically prefer warm weather
but when the air feels Jewishly chilly
I can't help but dive into every degree:

1. Caressing creamy, Jerusalem stones and mountainous
    terrain, uplifting all souls
2. Visiting the *Kotel* or *Har HaBayit*, life's climax, after a long
    period of absence
3. Jews like s'mores enveloped by the other, forming a circle,
    swaying at a *kumzits*
4. Seeing that singular Jew on the subway, or at your work,
    and exchanging smiles
5. Learning that a Jew aids POTUS, filling The White House
    with spirituality
6. Having *nitzulay shoah* beside IDF soldiers, fighting now for
    what they couldn't then
7. Standing by the birth of a Jewish baby, a new *neshama*
    lighting up a dim world
8. Watching the sea split in the Prince of Egypt & singing
    along to "when you believe"
9. Reading of an older man celebrate his bar-mitzvah & wrap
    tefillin for the first time
10. Marching in the Israeli Day Parade and having NYC stop,
    support, and wave

The View

While personal living spaces differ and divide
only the green and blue can capture our pride
gather us under one roof to celebrate the view
that takes our breath away
and graciously gives it back
so we can rave about its natural beauty
then RSVP, with a friend and a gift, to the next party

just this once
it is not what's on the inside
but the outside that counts

- *"Ma Rabu Ma'asecha Hashem"*

Shabbat Mornings

There is something special in the way the sun squeezes
through the shades, encourages my soul to gently cascade.
As sweet rugelach glisten beside the coffee
a week-long *DMC* starts with the Almighty.

A Jewish Melody

Inviting an aged voice to enter the circle
add to the dialogue teleporting through
generations, conducting confused breaths
on when to rise, when to fall, and when to feel.

Only by listening to the story of an old soul
can we transcend all physics and chemistry
revive a spirit draped in symphonies
that will one day come around and call on us
to join the circle and lead the orchestra.

-nigun

Find Yours

You are not what I thought a home would look like
because I didn't know what a real one was
until you brought boards and nails
hammers and hearts to the site
and built what I never found
to be so indestructible

-real *chevra*

Simply Syntax

There is a Master
Who creates priceless collections
and sends them down in search for each other.
It's simple
if each one was shaped and shined by the same Hand
then aren't miraculous works walking all over land?
Aren't they worth seeking
knowing
loving
without the command?
They are pieces of the Master
Masterpieces.

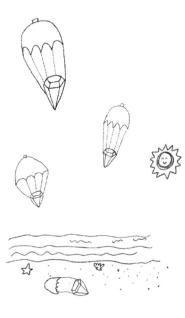

Section IV

Injury

The reality of *galut*, the exile and absence of the Beit Hamikdash, means we have a lot of history to unpack and homework to do as a people. In general, it's encouraged and commended when a Jew practices the teaching "מצוה גדולה להיות בשמחה תמיד" – it's a great mitzvah to be happy always. Yet there is a time and place for everything, as Shlomo Hamelech writes in Kohelet. In this section your sensitivities will be heightened and perspectives deepened. It's a place for Jewish injuries to hurt and heal, for faults to be acknowledged. We don't believe in perfection but we do believe in correction and *teshuva* being a lifelong journey.

The Exile

if only these tears worked as watercolors
they'd paint a face mural out of this misery

Taken

they've taken my dreams
forced them through a shredder
used its remains as confetti for parties
teardrops overflow baskets of candies

they've taken my breath
abused it to spin tornadoes of havoc
taking hope captive within its merciless winds
destroying any trace of a holiness, a conscience

the one thing they have not taken –
my soul

fools forever more
they've only sanctified me more

-victims of terrorism

Trouble in Paradise

It
is
simply
complicated

-Israeli politics

The Nine Days

9 months nourishing birth
9 days knowing death.
The irony of waking
with fresh wounds
surviving the questions
of every salty moon.

We cycle through traumas,
recycle grief alongside faith.
We inhale mortality
in return for
an exhale of immortality.

-the destruction

Bridging the Gap

it thrives in the in-betweens
it preys then

in-between faith and doubt
in-between love and loss
in-between light and dark
in-between
You
and
me

-yetzer hara

S.B.Y.

"Mazal tov! Soon by you."
I nod my head, fake a huge smile
while feeling the chills poke at me.
Once again I'm made more empty
left crippled by the *why* at the aisle.

Why "soon"?
This is what stings, burns my insides
to a crisp,
pulls it straight down to its knees as a beggar
begging the questions when alone in the dark.

Am I not made seamlessly, wholly in G-d's image?
Should I not be okay, be content with my own self?
Do I need my stomach to fill till it bleeds to be satisfied?
Do I need my heart to pound till it hurts to be worthy?
Do I need my head to host a zoo just to be happy?
Am I not something without the someone saying so?

I am not a half.
I am a whole.
I am not looking for a hero
I am looking for the one
who too sees one, not zero.

Together we will save the world
not as two halves but two wholes
tagging greater relationship goals –
a most powerful pair, force of souls.

-the real shidduch crisis

Women

I am not a barbie you can alter to your liking.
I am an altar you must be worthy of serving.

-we are sacred

Chained

Once upon a time
inside a beastly thing
laid chained hearts,
rusting and rattling
for years until one day
they forced its belly to gag
a mouthful of freedoms
and a million different drums
to escort them out as they dripped
in saliva and their new-founded selves.

-agunot

The Struggle is Real

you must see the struggle to serve G-d
bare your eyes & shatter the rose-colored glasses,
not everything is ash gray but neither is it flamingo pink,
experience the colors as they come without the filters
the way they have been produced upon the palette

-imo anochi b'tzara

Where?

You are everywhere
and in the nowhere

You are here and there
in the sea, earth, air

You are up and down
though it's a ghost town

You are right and left
even when cold & bereft

You are in and out
certainty slaving in doubt

You are all around
yet not found

I can't help but feel the thickening *kelipa*
strangling my sore longing for the *shechina*

-please, no more *hester panim*

Kavod Habriyot

Not dirty.
Indeed different.

-nations of the world

The Irony

wallets on strike, no cents to cough
students transfer out, some fall off
accounts on the brim, in bankruptcy
loose grip on tradition, spirituality

chinuch stapled to a dollar sign, pinned
onto a kid's chest & sent home thinned,
Torah access denied past the deadline
for the first time in 3 millennia – flattened
our national lifeline.

-absurd yeshiva tuition

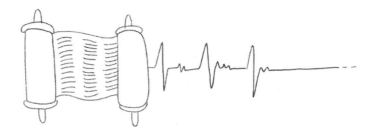

The Middle Path

lukewarm
my ideal temperature
there's nothing glorious in being burned or frozen
but when that's the case I'd rather drown in warm water
than surface to be surrounded by flames or bitten by frost

I've always lived with intensity
but now I'm dying for stability

-*machmir* isn't for everyone

The Window

Scraping a fallen sky
for a star teary-eyed,
not yet dulled
by the death toll,
to cry forth its light into a bunker's window
fill hope where every day's end lies hollow

A two paned glass witnessing
from the outside looking in
and inside looking out
the discoloration of day
the blinding of night
on savage repeat

Soaking the stench
of stacked bodies,
a face clear but never clean
of its ghastly fate,
yet that glimmer of light keeps trickling
crying through windows until it inspires

A rally of one
to become an Army of two
and a thunder of three
to become a Storm of four
and a body of five
to become a Nation of six

with fists breaking through
the window and barbed wire,
a phoenix raging and rising,
marching to the beat
of their beaten soul
toward a "never again"

today
as survivors in the morning wake
the sun is drawn a bit higher
as they bear another memory ache,
but with the brave batting of their lashes
they set the past and future world on fire

Yom Hazikaron

You can't teach someone how to sacrifice
it's built-in
the need to sweat
the need to serve
for something you can't point to
for a nation promised to be immortal

though the state of forever comes at a cost
with no discount, no refund
a price given value
but don't be mistaken

a life for a life
is not an eye for an eye
a soul for a soul
is the story of *Am Yisrael*
a life full of soul
a soul full of sacrifice

a sacrifice full of life

99

BD"E

Even during the *shiva*
wholeness weaves through
sewing together the sobs
of souls ripped at the seams.

Because of Adam and Eve
seven days plummet
down and down and down
until the bottom of rock bottom.

Because of G-d
seven days rise
up and up and up
until there is full comfort, closure.

We will find life again
not now
not never
but again.

-aveilut

The Tablets

The gravity of those *luchot* - broken – is what granted us
forgiveness.
Let's not be ashamed of owning each scattered and severed
piece.
It is precisely what made Hashem fall in love, making our
bond unbreakable.

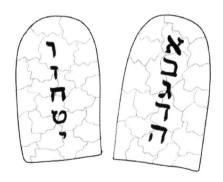

Raba Emunatecha

Don't break down by your sins, break free because of them.
Don't break up with yourself, break into yourself.

-breaking is becoming

Emunah

you can call on the
ponds
lakes
rivers
oceans
the waters of every body
and still it will never be enough
to quench the thirst of a soul dehydrated
from running marathons it's not ready for
trying to replenish but ending up with a faith
fractured more

-pace yourself

Judaism vs. Jews

Sometimes I feel as if I live a double life.
I'm just a Jew, not Judaism exactly.
I pray, though often cannot hear my whisperings.
I kosher eat and do but don't feel different.
I'm one of many souls that practice day and night
yet does my Jewishness spark any dynamite?

Misconceptions

1. All Israeli music is religious music
2. All Hasidic men are shtark *bachurim*
3. All hair coverings are clunky & itchy
4. All Bais Yaakov girls are narrow-minded
5. All IDF soldiers are spotless and mighty
6. All Chabad houses are practically perfect
7. All of Tanach is an adventurous fairy tale
8. All Jewish organizations are innocent

9. All *mitzvot* are dull and difficult
10. All Orthodox authors & artists are *nebby*
11. All Jewish guys are too short or too quiet
12. All Jews speak Yiddish, Hebrew, & English
13. All Jewish girls are Oscar-winning yentas
14. All Jews are white, rich, and snobby
15. All Israelis are rough, spicy, and nosy
16. All Jews have the same political views
17. All Jews litter & wreak havoc everywhere

18. All Jews are in business, medicine, or law
19. All Friday/shabbos prep is hectic & dramatic
20. All Jewish foods are too oily, salty, or sweet

Pesach Prep

the whiff of cleaning solution
up it does clean but not solve
the impact of days scrubbed down
packed tightly with anxieties
holding you accountable
for every hour spent
not wearing gloves
not washing walls
not throwing out
not making kosher
everything
from
sky
to
earth

-what the holiday has become

Sincerely

Dear Hashem,

You should know, I appreciate what You do for me. It's just hard
being a soul in a physical body, an infinite piece of You living in the
confined spaces of me. Today was not how I wanted it to go in the
slightest, but how can I complain? Yet I do so in the mostest. You let
me live another day with my faculties intact and blessed me in ways
making me think it's all my doing. It's really because of You, the good,
the bad, and the things we can't name. Even more, You revealed
Yourself to Avraham, You enabled Sarah to have a baby, You helped
Rivka succeed in swapping the *brachot*, You gave Yitzchak strength for
the *akeidah*, You gave Leah a second chance at love, You heard and
answered Rachel's prayers, and You saved Yaakov from Eisav. These
things happened back then but is no less part of the journey that
brought me to this point in time, where I constantly contemplate
ma'aseh avot siman l'banim. Maybe their stories are intertwined with
mine. Maybe there are no endings but beginnings because of that. My
avot and *imahot* merited miracles as did their descendants leaving
mitzrayim. Can You perform them now too? For me? Please? Can You
reveal Yourself to me, grant me a family, show me the path to success,
build my stamina, bless me with true love, hear and answer my
prayers, offer me salvation and redemption? I'm tired of swimming
and treading until my limbs go numb. Like the Jew wrapped by the
Yam Suf, can You wrap me too? Can You split it once more?
The sea for me?

From the depths,

-Your child

Call Me

Rabbi

Rebbe

Rav

Rebbi

Moreh

Mashgiach

Av Bayit

Tzaddik

Menahel

Rebbetzin

Tzadeikes

Morah

Em Bayit

Mashgicha

Menahelet

Rabbanit

Mashiach

A Yid.

-A Simple Jew

Yom Kippur Reflections

The peeks and stares
The smiles with whispered swears
a charade we perpetuate

The likes and looks
The hands with hidden hooks
things we don't appreciate

The mads and hatters
The meals with secret chatters
pampered egos we inflate

The high fives and hugs
The listening with plugs
relationships we don't authenticate

Good reflections are hard to find.
Great reflections are harder to maintain.
Soul reflections are the rarest of them all yet innate.

I Ought

I ought to know there's all too much to grow
to truly understand the natural hand
that stretches out in glee, inviting me
to plow and plant and reap the seeds I sow.

I ought to chime there's all too little time
to truly look within, ask how I've been
that shakes my hair to know I'm not aware
to joyfully journeying up the climb.

I ought to say there's all too much to pray
to truly heal the broken spinning wheel
that turns in hope while washing soil with soap
to rest and right the wrongs, will good outweigh?

-120 years may not be enough

Section V

Mind

The brain and heart are a powerful duo making up who we are, but it's not complete without the mind. Being Jewish means breathing the values of education. The text is not merely what we crave, it is the understanding of its application which decorates our daily lives. *Matan Torah* gave our nation a pulse and Torah study is what kept it alive since. Our community revolves dearly around learning and teaching, making it a mutual and timeless relationship. In this section you can put that Yiddishe *kop* (head) into practice with thought-provoking ideas and a fresh look at ancient beliefs that are as alive and relevant today as they were when given.

Siyum

Every *megillah* starts with a single word

Colorful

hu-man
man with a hue
many hues
even when our innermost worlds are eclipsing
we are warriors of colors, all brilliantly blending

The Sage

The body is smart,
the mind is sharp,
though after much
is felt and thought,
the soul is most wise
for it knows the not yet taught,
books not yet bought
bent into shape,
words not yet wrestled
tackled by the tongue,
blanks not yet smoothed
made into sense,
ideas not yet caught
cooked by hope.

Torah *U'mada*

Torah *U'mada*
l'havdil, the Jewish Hannah Montana.
The best of both worlds always rocking
where the Modox continues on flocking.
Spearheaded by the "Rav" – Soloveitchik
a great light grown from one waxed wick.
Where science and spirituality meet for coffee
melting into the other as sweet & warm toffee.
While the concepts of art & methods of math don't dictate
they're agents trained to unlock upper worlds via its gate.
To elevate the mundane you must engage with it
infuse holy teachings to raise its grounded spirit.
It's not a magic trick but a journey taken day by day
like *tremp* drivers going an extra mile out of the way
to see things with an added lens, enhancing vision all around,
to hear things at a higher frequency, sharpening every sound.
It's a movement founded on courageous risk, not recklessness
dreaming to merge the two worlds that give more, never less.
While you can either support, stand neutral or oppose,
what you follow is fine, just be sure it's you who chose.

The Rabbi

A wizard's wand
not a one size fits all
the call of duty it goes beyond.

Some are bent
some are straight
wholly heaven sent.

They work their magic
when working for the One Above
holding the magic's magic.

The Dumbledore beard
everyone once loved
modernity labels weird.

But we can bring back the fad
if we first see their textiles
not as plain but plaid.

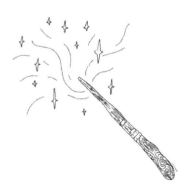

Olam Hazeh

Judaism can seem like a combo series of no's, *assur's* and don'ts in this world. Though it's merely a menu laying out the all-you-can-eat buffet, the yes's, in the next.

-a corridor to *olam haba*

The Party

Some days feel like a party I never planned or wanted to attend.
The music thumps too loud, it's hard to choose a direction. The floor is
covered in spilled drinks pinning down my steps, it's hard to walk. The
people barely breathe from deep belly laughs, it's hard to talk. I'm seen as
the party pooper brushing down decorations with each blink of an eye.
But that's not my intention. I'm just floating around trying to find
the purpose I once had here.

I keep passing familiar faces every few turns, swapping cheap smiles.
I keep hoping for a miracle to pop out of a drawer with a sign reading:
"you will arrive at your destination in two more feet on the right",
since I've always walked with my two, *emunah*-filled feet down.
I keep pouring chips onto my plate trying to fit in, feel normal.
But what could possibly be different at this fork in the road, in the kitchen
at this party?

Everyday used to be like the next, spiraling through me at the same
momentum. Then time decided to mature and pocket predictability,
stability for itself. I'm left here with inches of uncertainty. I'm left to be a
nomad searching for a ripened rhyme and reason. I'm living between these
anxious weeks, these parties on replay with a lost and frustrated pulse.

And when it seems as if hope has forgotten my address, it comes flaring at
the window. Hope lowers the music, washes the floor, and "shh"s the
people. An image of a calm, colorful future comes to mind and a mantra:
"until then, *l'chaim!*" Hope reassures, although life is a party I didn't plan
my way or want to attend solo, I must enjoy the time I have to sit in the
middle of everything and not worry about anything. I must dance as if no
one is watching, before I enter the world's business where that's all they do.
I must appreciate my plate before I become the one who serves and cleans
them. I must learn to say *l'chaim* even within the noisy unknown and use my
two hands and feet filled with *emunah* to raise a glass and sing aloud "until
then, *l'chaim!*"

Your Effort is Enough

Lungs. They filter through every intention until reaching those righteous ones. We don't give them enough credit. They bring exactly enough oxygen to the bloodstream so no matter what the pollution is like outside, we'll be ready. We do our *hishtadlut* and then breathe, regardless of the results.

Connections in High Places

They say it's not what you know, it's who you know.
And they're right.

-knowing the *Ribono Shel Olam*

Ge'avah vs. Anavah

Flats are not immature, neither are stilettos too much.
Quiet humility is as chic as blatant *bitachon*.
There's a time for both in their rightful amount - a *mida* for
each *midda*. There's a reason *ge'avah* and *anavah* are separated
by few letters. They are bridges to be crossed with the right
practice, patience, and pair of shoes.

Two-Faced

a saw that cuts but isn't seeing
a watch that tells but isn't watching
a plate that feeds but isn't plating
a book that sells but isn't booking
a face that looks but isn't facing
like a please that asks but isn't pleasing
nor thanking

-*chutzpah* treads a fine line

Puzzle Pieces

King and judge
Prophet and priest
Forgive and grudge
Fast and feast
Commandment and exemption
Sinner and beggar
Exile and redemption
Richer and pauper

No matter
who and what
where and when
we need
one and the other

When?

Today can always say tomorrow while tomorrow will look bewildered at yesterday and think "why not today"?

-im lo achshav eymatai

Kamocha

Hillel summed up the entirety of Torah on one leg with this
principle. I don't think it would be wild to say the greatest
service you can do for the world is to love yourself more, not
less. It's about the *kamocha*. You are a mirror onto yourself and
others. If you don't polish it every day how can you possibly
see correctly? Hashem intended for you:
to embrace *kamocha*, not erase
to befriend *kamocha*, not defriend
to pamper *kamocha*, not hamper
to love *kamocha*, not shove

to love *kamocha* unconditionally
because He does religiously

-self-care/love

The Barista

He is the Big Barista brewing in the shop upstairs
making coffee creations for various state of affairs,
mixing things in the global cup where swirls of all sorts meet
saturating the daily atmosphere with a natural bitter & sweet.

They're always designed to perfection
an awe-filled reflection,
but on some days it'll be hard to see
the shapes made by the Almighty,
with blessings contoured through
alongside a heavenly ombre hue.

Even if you don't often identify
the seamless art swimming by,
it is there in its rightful drip
waiting for you to take that first sip.

Who's Rich?

i count all the things not belonging to me
anchor their absence
then set them free to the sea
with my intoxicating envy

-hasameach b'chelko

Unknown

Knowing the much
grasping the little,
the clock's a crutch
its ticks go brittle

Tells of a when
no sign of a what,
anti-man's ken
missing the real putt

Makes one believe
learning is losing,
a "known" meets eve
as "un" is rising

The unknown shines
passing through the years,
as time confines
filling it with fears

Why so shallow?
rushing to know lots,
while still hollow
like bows without knots

As the depth lends
the clock strikes midnight,
true knowing scends
to a grateful height

For grasping the little "un" floods a sea so great
while the much "known" always flows to an empty strait

-true *chochma*

129

All I Know

All I know is that I don't know what I don't know
and that knowing is all I will ever fully know.

All I feel are the many feelings that only always feel
and not the feelings that don't feel what they don't feel.

All I see are the things which I see that I don't see
and that seeing is the only see I need not see.

-bina

Shalom Aleichem

That "*shalom aleichem*" shake and smile get me every time.
Despite it not being a long while, there's no crime
in asking and answering for the tenth time in a day.
Though I ready my lips for its usual Olympics, I know to say:
"*Baruch Hashem*", "*Yishtabach Shemo*", "*Toda la-El*"!
These words have gone the distance, travelled far too well,
but am I aware of what they mean? Do I believe them?
Are they just another easy trim? A quickly done hem?
Are they fancy acrobatic tricks and flexible moves
to ensure everyone I come in contact with approves?

131

Possible vs. Perfect

We are not a perfect people.
We are all that's possible, and more.

Sizing Up

people are petite
deeds are small
days are medium
problems are large
Chasdei Hashem is extra large
Hashem – we don't carry that size

Tzedaka

When you give
know when to start
when to pause
and continue

know the source
the offspring
and nutritional supply

know the why
and the how
but not the who

Read All About It!

As the headlines have shown
we don't smoothly sail by,
we make a splash
a wave
a tsunami of change,
so sailors years from now
can feel the ripples in their feet
moving them forward
along the ruffled waters
wondering how it all came to be.
Who birthed the sea? What was her wild story?

Glossary

Achdus – unity

Agunot – women chained to dead marriages, stuck without a "get"

Ahavah – love

Akeidah – the binding of Isaac

Amidah – the Shemoneh Esrei, a silent prayer standing with feet together

Am Yisrael – the Jewish nation

Anavah – humility

Arba'at Haminim – the four species used on sukkot

Assur's – prohibitions

Av Bayit – the appointed father figure for a yeshiva or seminary

Aveilut – mourning

Avodah – the work done in the Temple

Avot – forefathers

Bachurim – yeshiva guys

Baruch Hashem – blessed be the Name

Besamim – the spices used for havdalah

Bina – understanding

Birkat Kohanim – the priestly benediction

Bitachon – trust

Brachot – blessings

Bris – circumcision

Bubby/Savta – grandmother

B'tzelem Elokim – in G-d's image

Café Kar – cold coffee

Chagim – holidays

Chametz – leavened foods forbidden on Pesach

Chaping – Yiddish for "understanding"

Charif – spicy

Charoset – sweet relish made from nuts and fruit, one of the symbolic foods at the Pesach seder

Chasdei Hashem – G-d's kindness or grace

Chavayot – experiences

Chavrusa/Talmid/Rebbe – partner, student, teacher

Chavrusa – study partner or companion
Chesed – kindness or giving
Chevra – society or friend group
Chidush – new insight
Chinuch – education or discipline
Chochma – wisdom
Chol Hamoed – the middle weekdays of the festivals
Chuppah – wedding canopy
Chutzpah – gall or nerve
Derech – path or way
DMC – deep, meaningful conversation
Eidot – groups or camps
Em Bayit – the appointed mother figure for a seminary
Emes – truth
Emunah – faith
Erech – worth or value
Gashmiyut – materialism
Ge'avah – haughtiness
Gematria – interpreting Hebrew scriptures through a numerological code
Hagbah – lifting of the Torah scroll
Hakarat Hatov – "recognizing the good", showing appreciation
Hamalach Hagoel – recited after the shema in bed
Hamentaschen – a triangular-filled pastry baked for Purim
Har – "הר סיני", Mt. Sinai
Har Habayit – the Temple Mount
Hasameach B'Chelko – "one who is happy with their portion", Pirkei Avot 4:1
Hashgacha Pratit – divine providence
Hatikvah – "the hope", Israel's national anthem
Hatzlacha U'Bracha – success and blessing
Havay Dan Et Kol Adam L'Kaf Z'Chut – a commandment to judge your fellow favorably
Havdalah – "separation", religious ceremony marking the end of shabbat
Heimish – very Jewish, homey
Hester Panim – concealed face of G-d

Hishtadlut – effort

Hitbodedut – meditation or self-solitude

Hodu L'Hashem Ki Tov – "praise the Lord for He is good", Pslams 118:1

Imahot – foremothers

Im Lo Achshav Eymatai – "if not now, when?", Pirkei Avot 1:14

Imo Anochi B'Tzara – "I am with him in distress", Psalms 91:15

Kamocha – "like yourself", sourced from "ואהבת לרעך כמוך"

Kavod Habriyot – "honor G-d's creations", human dignity

Kehila – community or congregation

Kelipa – "peel", in Kabbala terms it describes evil or distance from G-d

Ketonet – coat or shirt

Kibud Av V'Em – commandment to respect one's mother and father

Kiddush Levana – sanctifying the new moon

Kinderlach – Yiddish for "children"

Kiruv – Jewish outreach

Kohen Gadol – the High Priest

Kol Yisrael Areivim Zeh L'Zeh – all Jews are responsible for one another

Kotel – western wall

Kumzits – musical gathering where people sit and sing

Lashon Hara – "evil tongue", derogatory speech

Layn – reading from the Torah during the prayer service

L'Chaim – a toast meaning "to life"!

L'havdil – showing a distinction between something great and of lesser status

Luchot – the tablets, "לוחות הברית"

Machloket L'Shem Shamayim – an argument for the sake of Heaven

Machmir – stringent (in halachic matters or positions)

Ma'aseh Avot Siman L'Banim – the actions of our forefathers/mothers are a sign for the (future) children

Ma Rabu Ma'asecha Hashem – "how great, many are Your deeds Hashem", Psalms 104:24

Mashgiach – "supervisor", someone who supervises the kashrut of a kitchen/establishment

Mashgicha – a female supervisor

Mechitzah – "partition", separate sections for men and women at religious functions

Megillah – any of the five books or scrolls in Ketuvim

Menahel – a principal or director

Menahelet – a female principal or director

Mida – measurement or amount

Midda – character trait (pl. middot)

Mishpacha – family

Mitpachat – a headscarf in Hebrew

Mitzrayim – Egypt

Mitzvot – commandments or deeds

Modeh ani – "I give thanks", the prayer recited upon waking

Morah – female teacher

Moreh – male teacher

Mussar – ethical teaching or instruction

Na'aseh V'nishma – "we will do and we will listen"

Nebby – Yiddish slang for "poor" or "dorky"

Nefesh – "living soul", the spiritual existence residing in the body

Neitz – "Hanetz Hachamah", sunrise/earliest time to say Shemoneh Esrei

Nekuda Tova – a good aspect or point

Neshama – soul (pl. neshamot)

Nigun – religious song or tune

Nitzulay Shoah – holocaust survivors

Olam Haba – the world to come

Olam Hazeh – this world

Oneg – pleasures of shabbat

Pasuk – verse

Payis – Yiddish way to say "peot"

Peot – Hebrew for sidelocks or sideburns

Pushka – Yiddish for "tzedaka box"

Raba Emunatecha – great is your faithfulness, sourced from "מודה אני"

Rabbeinu Tam – usually the stricter halachic opinion (keeping shabbat for longer)

Ratzon – will

Reut – friendship

Ribono Shel Olam – Master of the Universe

Saba – grandfather

Shalom Aleichem – "peace be upon you", a greeting between people

Shalom – goodbye

Shamayim – sky or heaven

Shanah Habah – next year in Jerusalem, "שנה הבאה בירושלים"

Shechina – the divine presence

Shiva – the seven-day mourning period

Shofar – ram's horn used as a trumpet

Shoko B'Sakit – Israeli chocolate milk in a bag

Shomer – keep or safeguard

Shtreimel – a fur hat worn by married, Haredi men

Shuk – marketplace

Shylah – Yiddish way to say "she'elah" (usually a halachic one), Hebrew for "question"

Siddur – prayer book

Simcha – happiness

Siyum – "completion", a celebration of a completed unit of Torah study

Slicha – "sorry" or "excuse me"

Tefillah – prayers

Tefillin – phylactery

Temidiyut – consistency

Teshuva – "to return", repentance

Toda La-El – thank the Lord

Torah Sh'Beal Peh U'Bichtav – the Oral Law and Written Law

Torah U'mada – Torah and science or secular knowledge

Tremp – hitchhike

Tzaddik – a righteous or holy person

Tzadeikes – a woman who is righteous

Tzedaka – charity

Tzitzit – religious garb with knotted fringes

U'vnei – "and their offspring", "וזכני לגדל בנים ובני בנים"

V'ahavta L'rayacha Kamocha – commandment to love your neighbor as you love yourself

Vayehi Or – "and there was light", Genesis 1:3

V'zakeini L'gadel - "may I merit to raise", "וזכני לגדל בנים ובני בנים"
Yam Suf - the Reed Sea
Yarmulkes - Yiddish for "kippahs", translated as skullcap
Yetzer Hara - evil inclination
Yirah - fear or awe
Yishtabach Shemo - may His Name be praised
Yom Hazikaron - Israeli Memorial Day
Yom Ha'atzmaut - Israeli Independence Day
Yom Yerushalayim - a day celebrating the liberation and unification of
Jerusalem
Zaidy - Yiddish for grandfather
Zerizut - alacrity
Zmirot - hymns

Made in the USA
Middletown, DE
07 February 2023